Cat Unicorn
Coloring Book

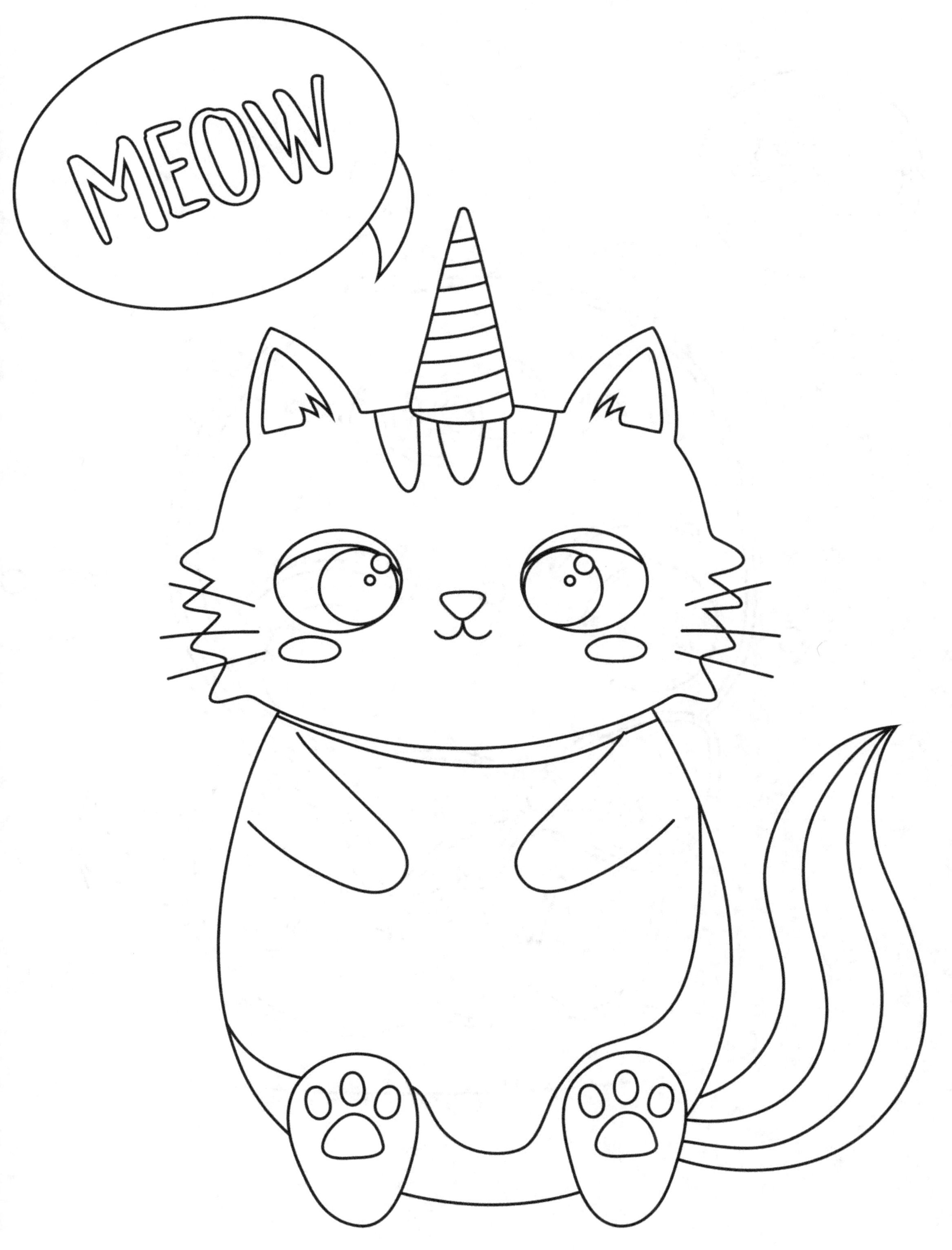
MEOW

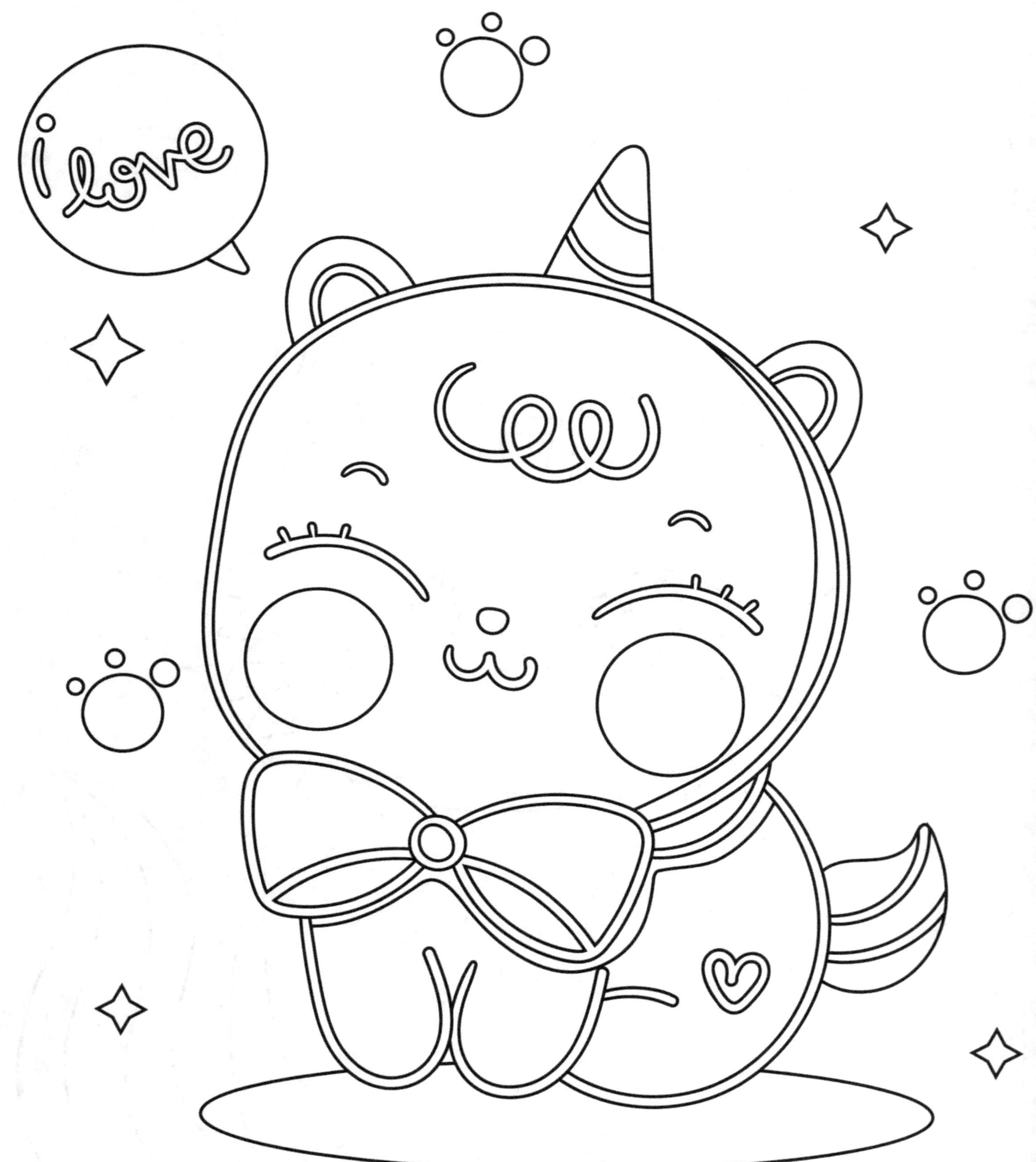

i love

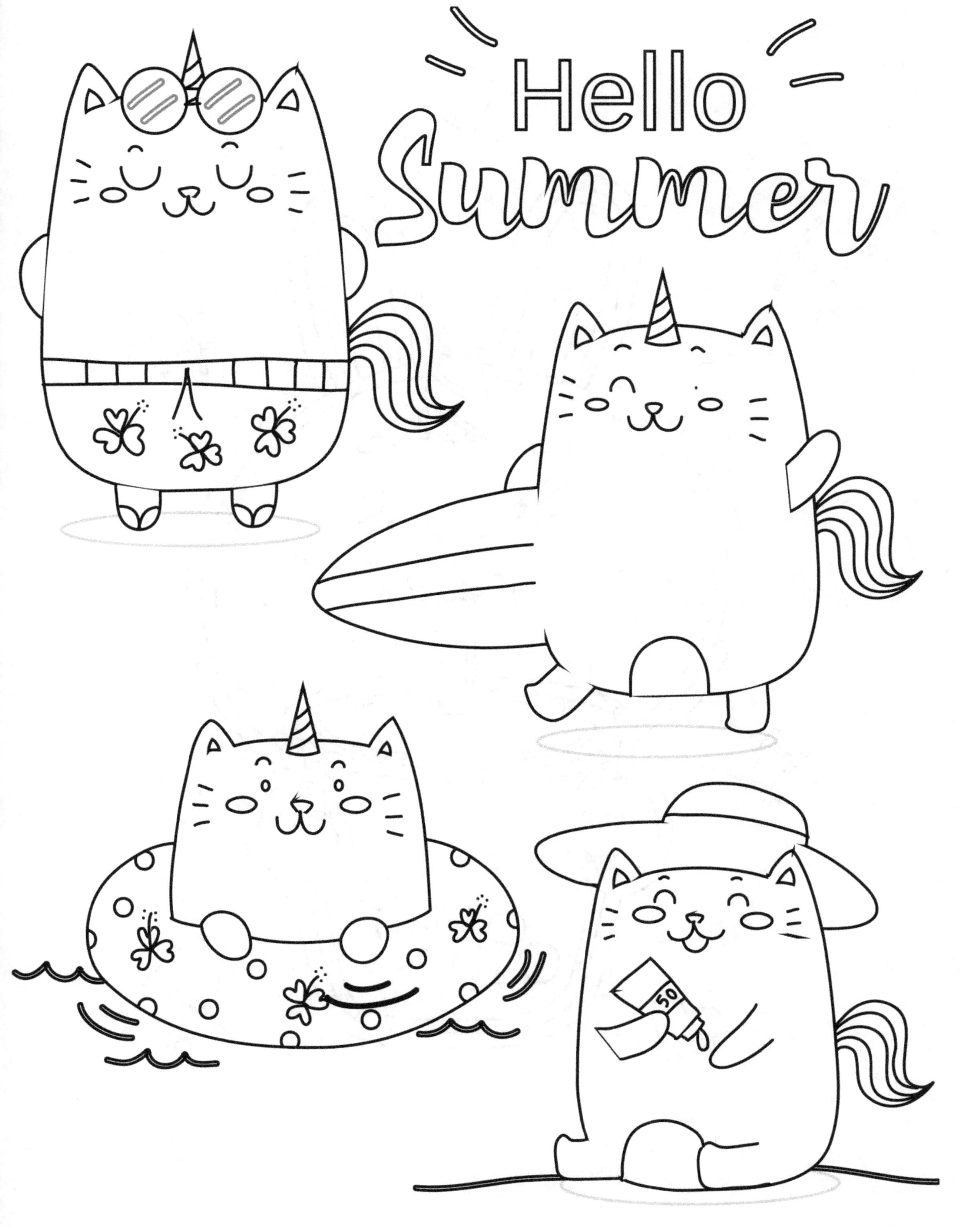

Hello Summer

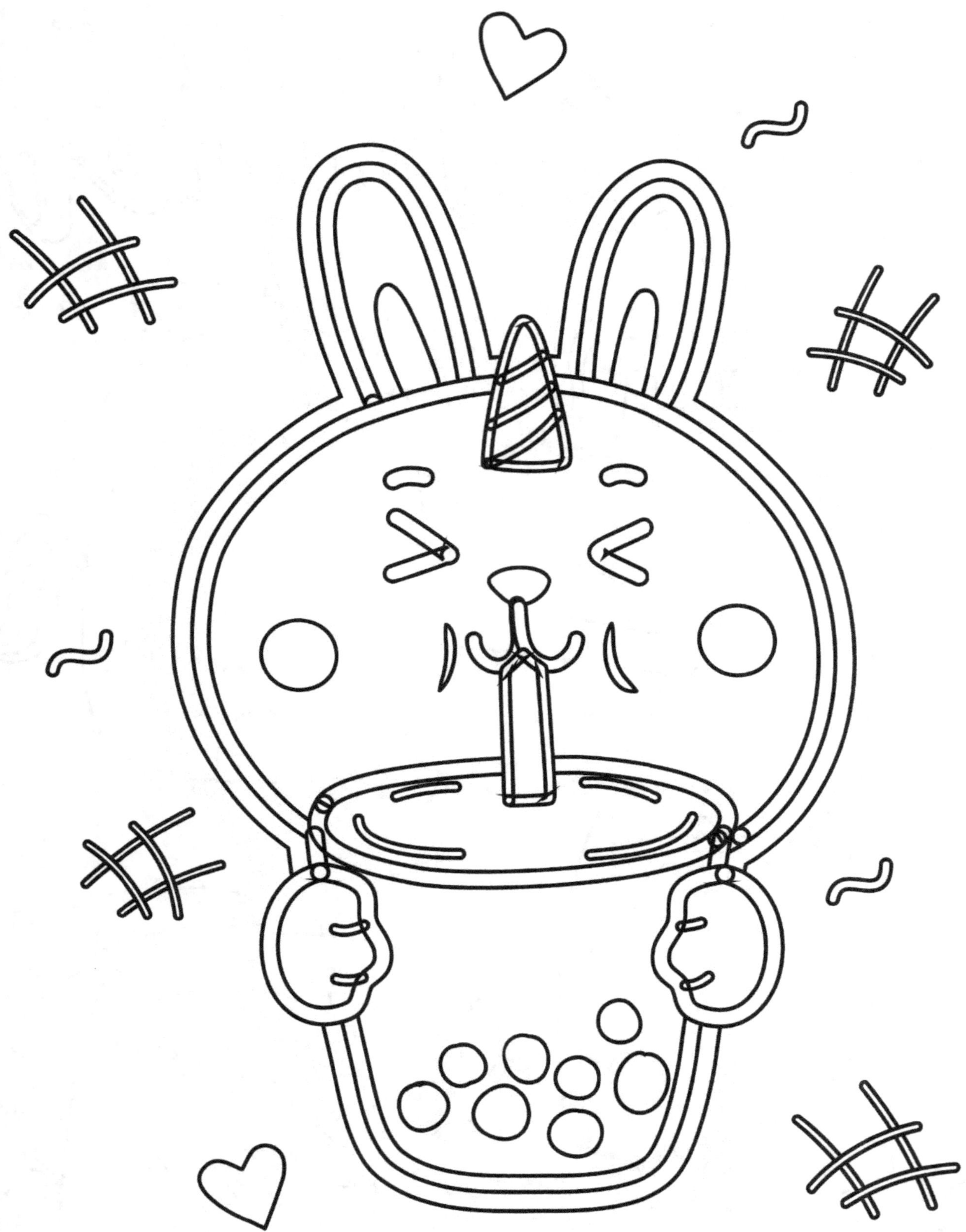

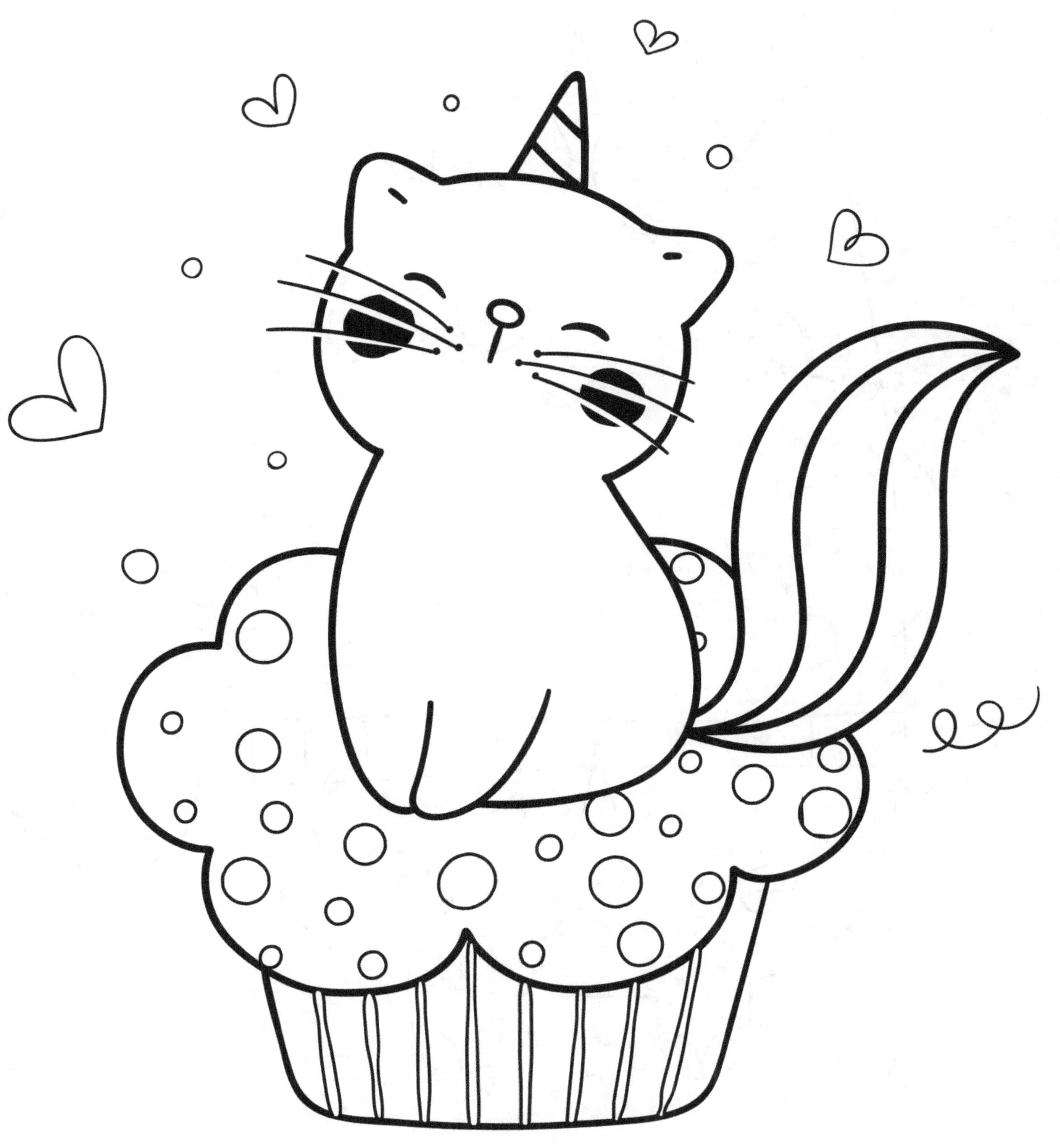

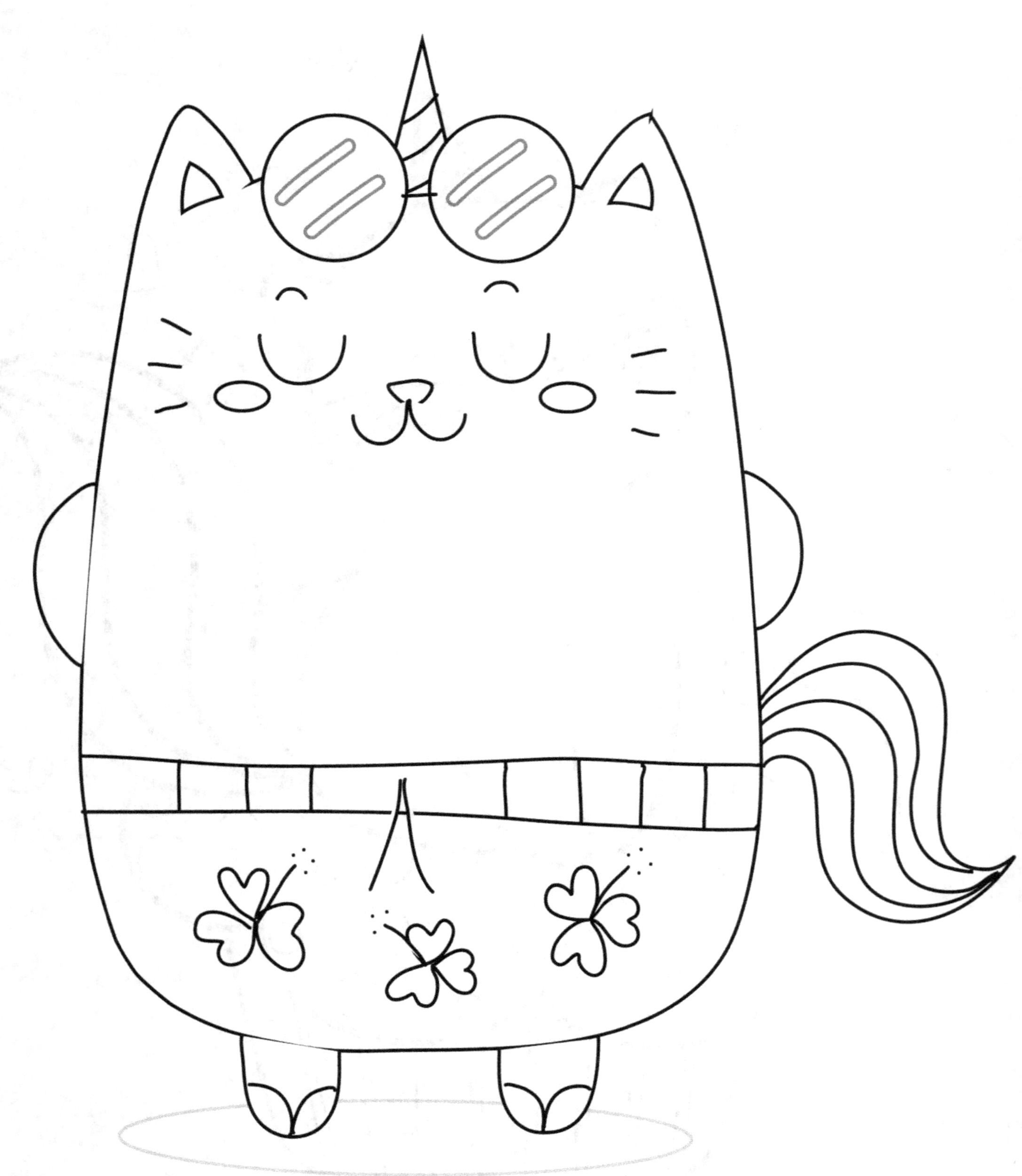

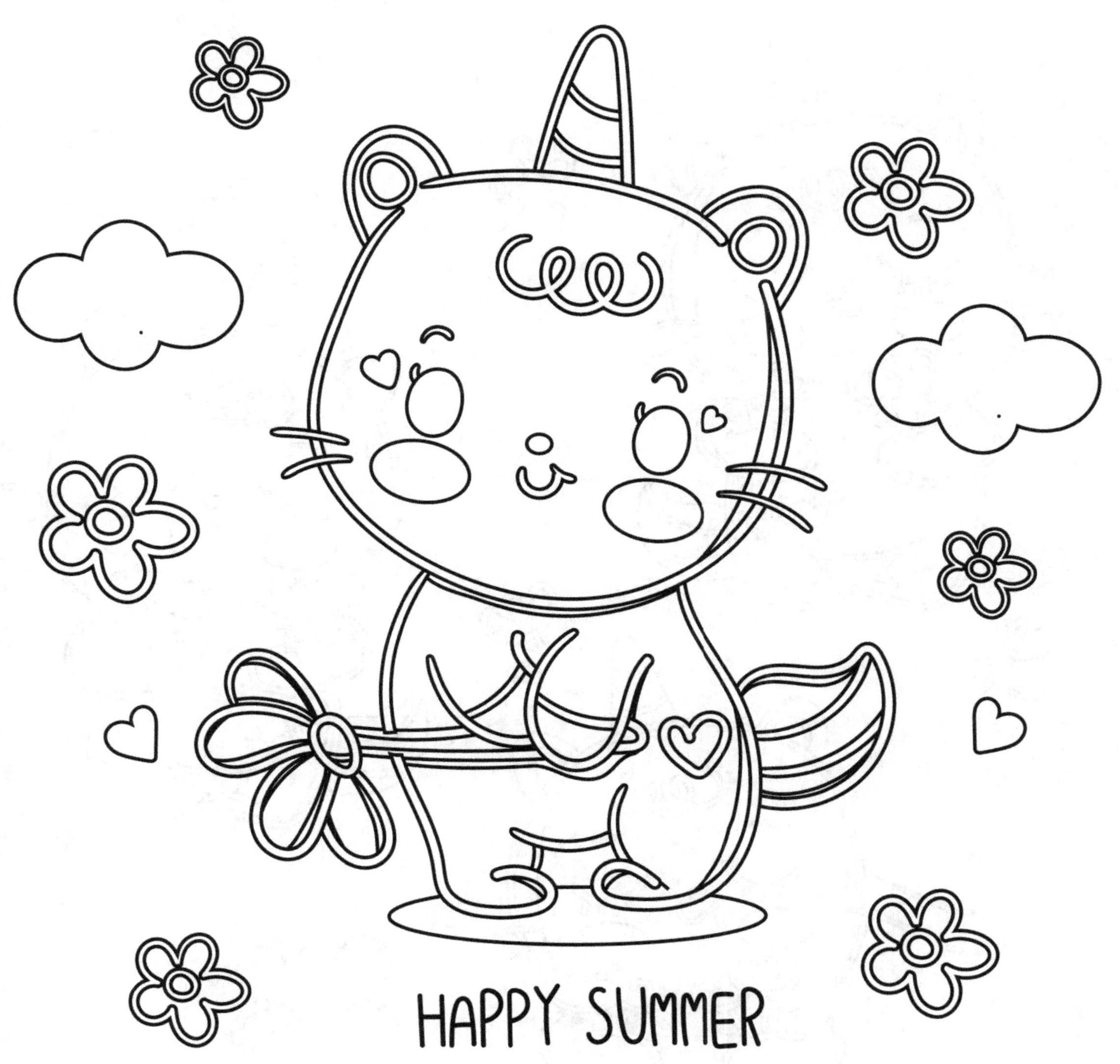
HAPPY SUMMER

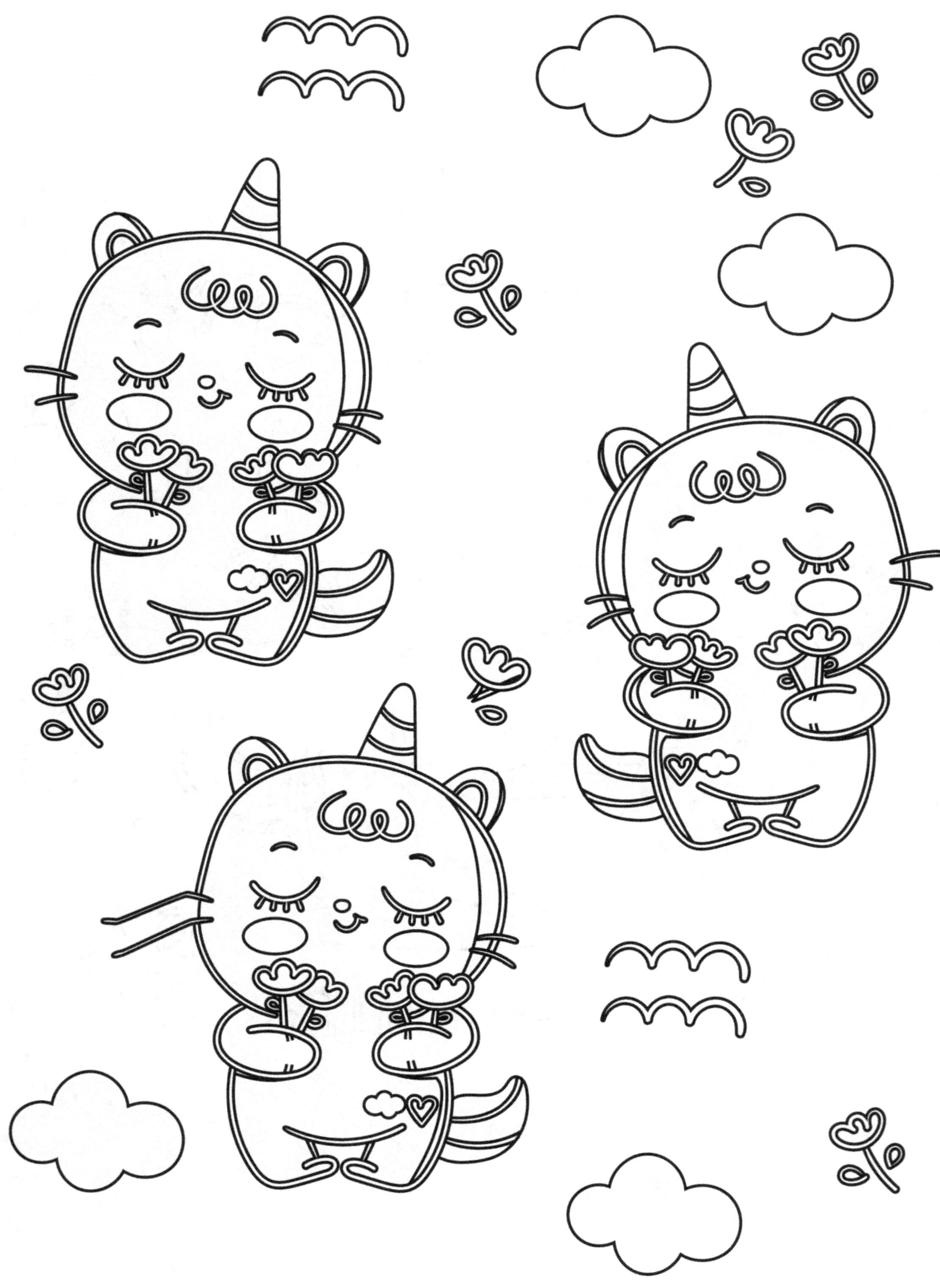

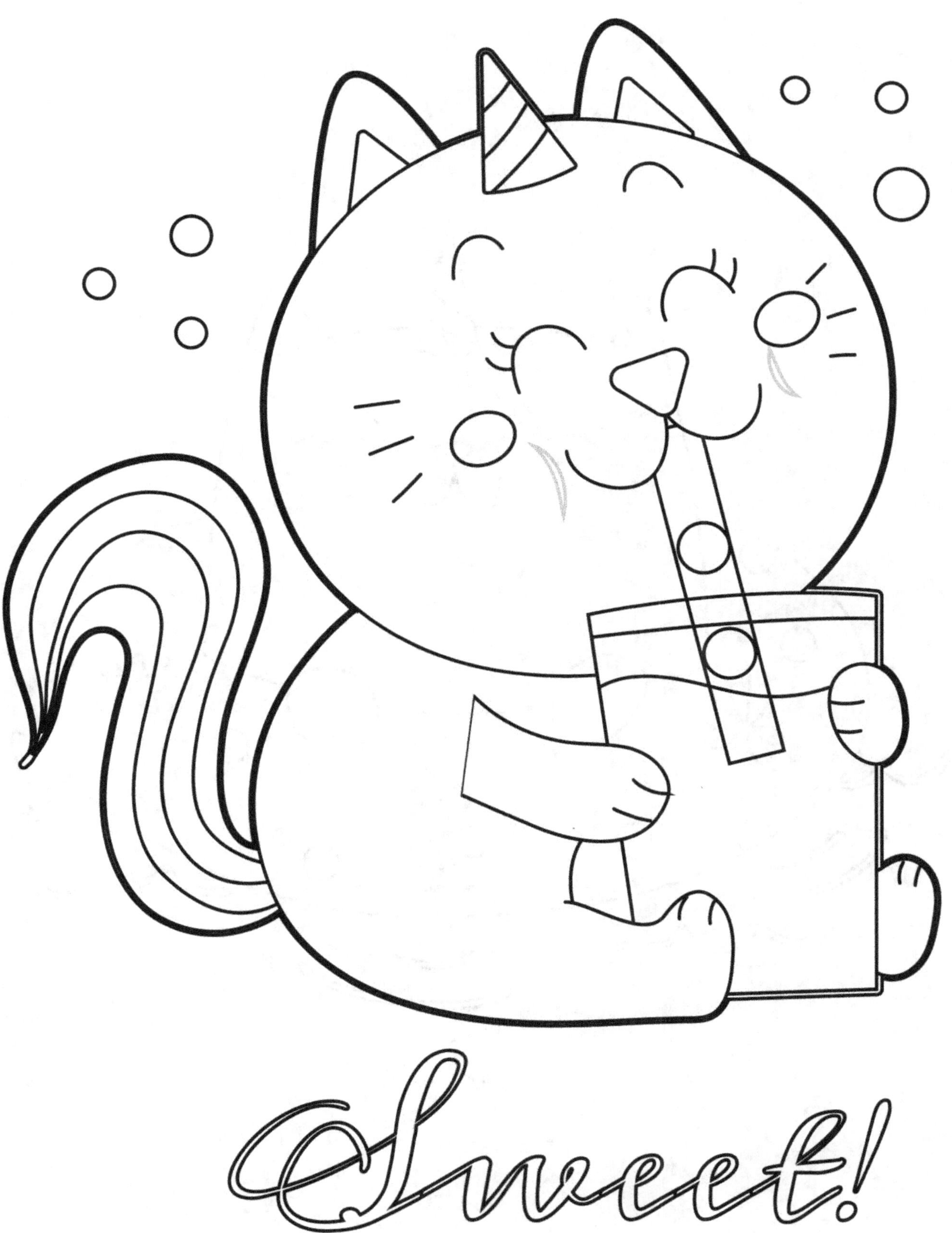

Sweet!

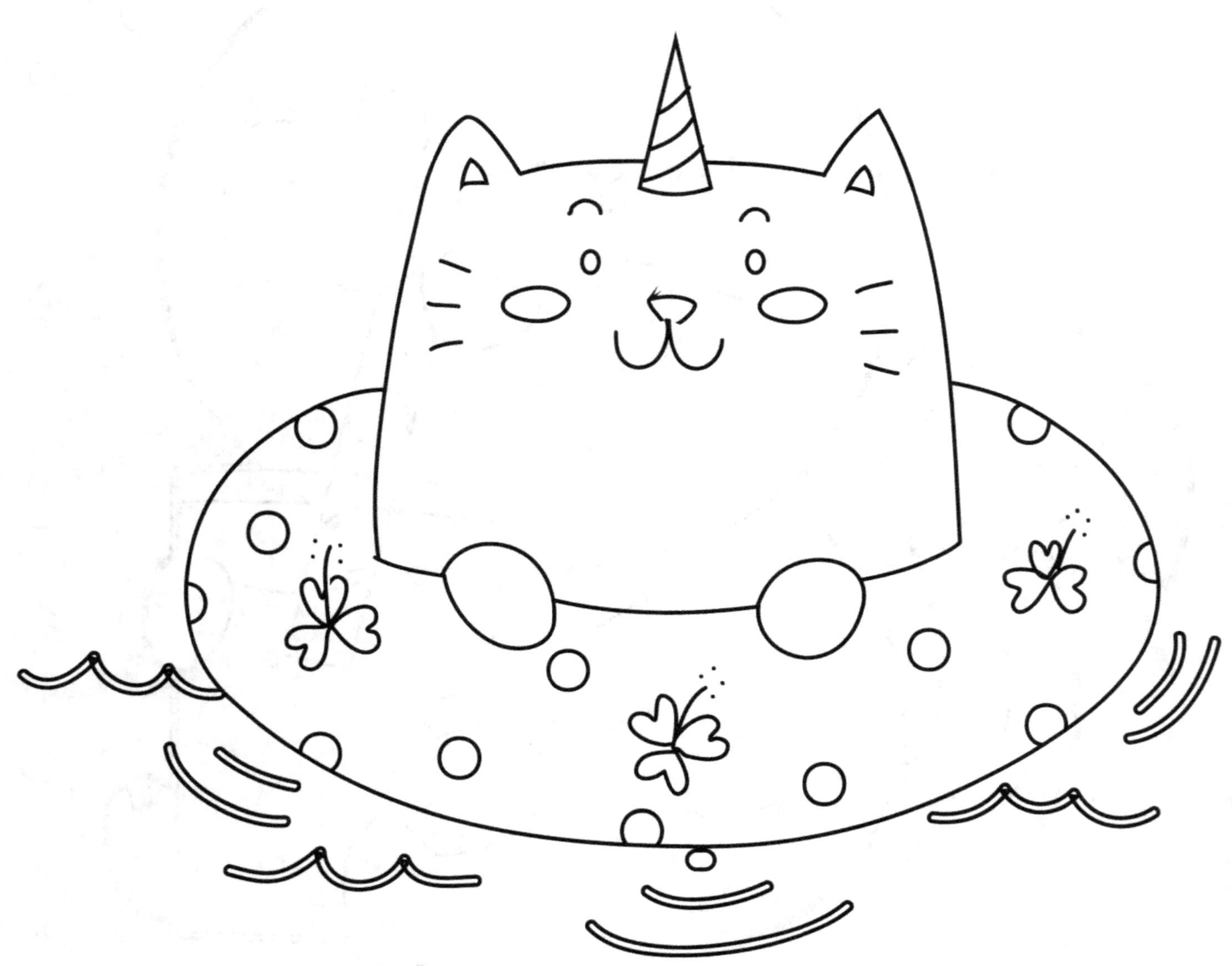

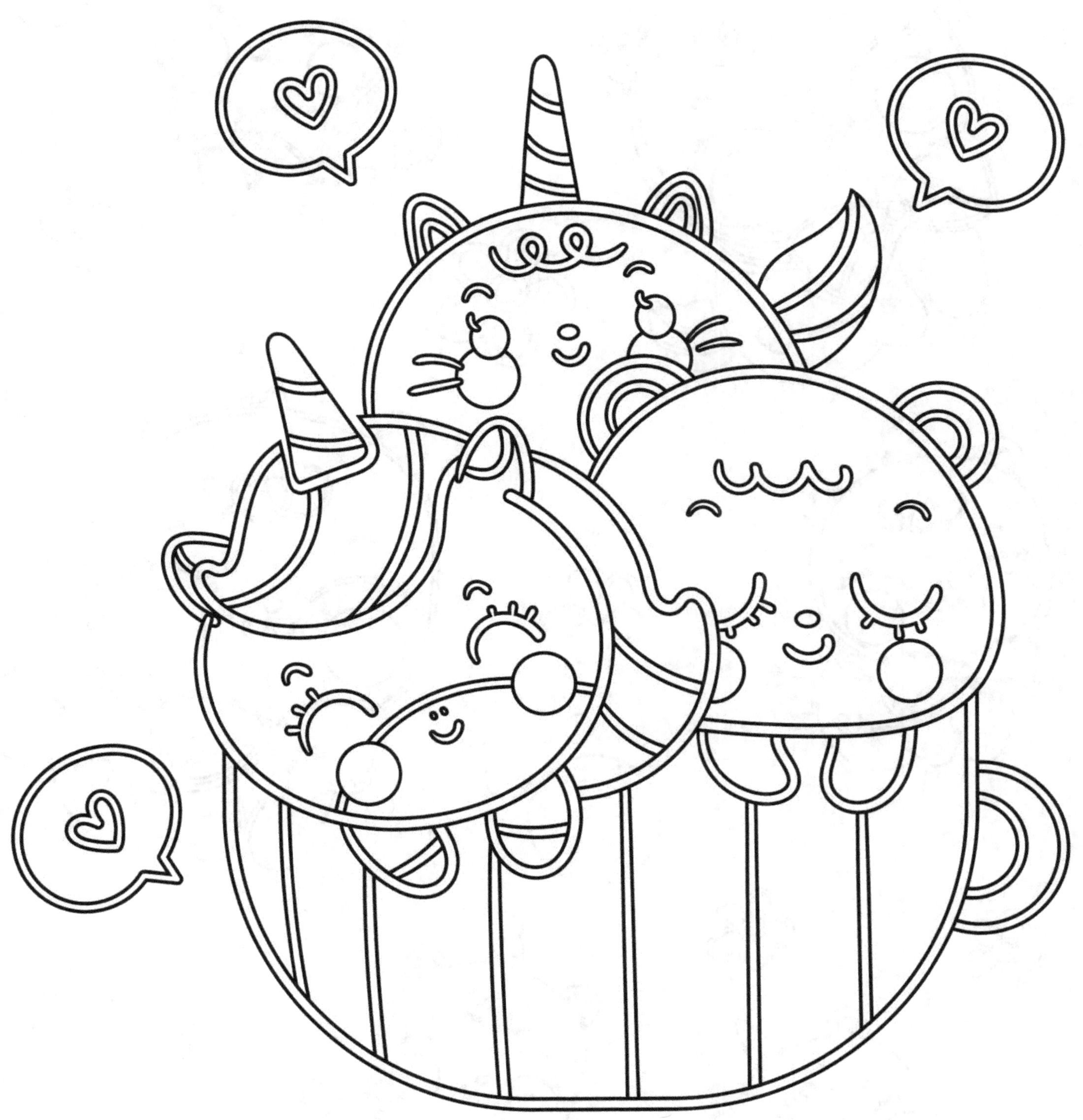

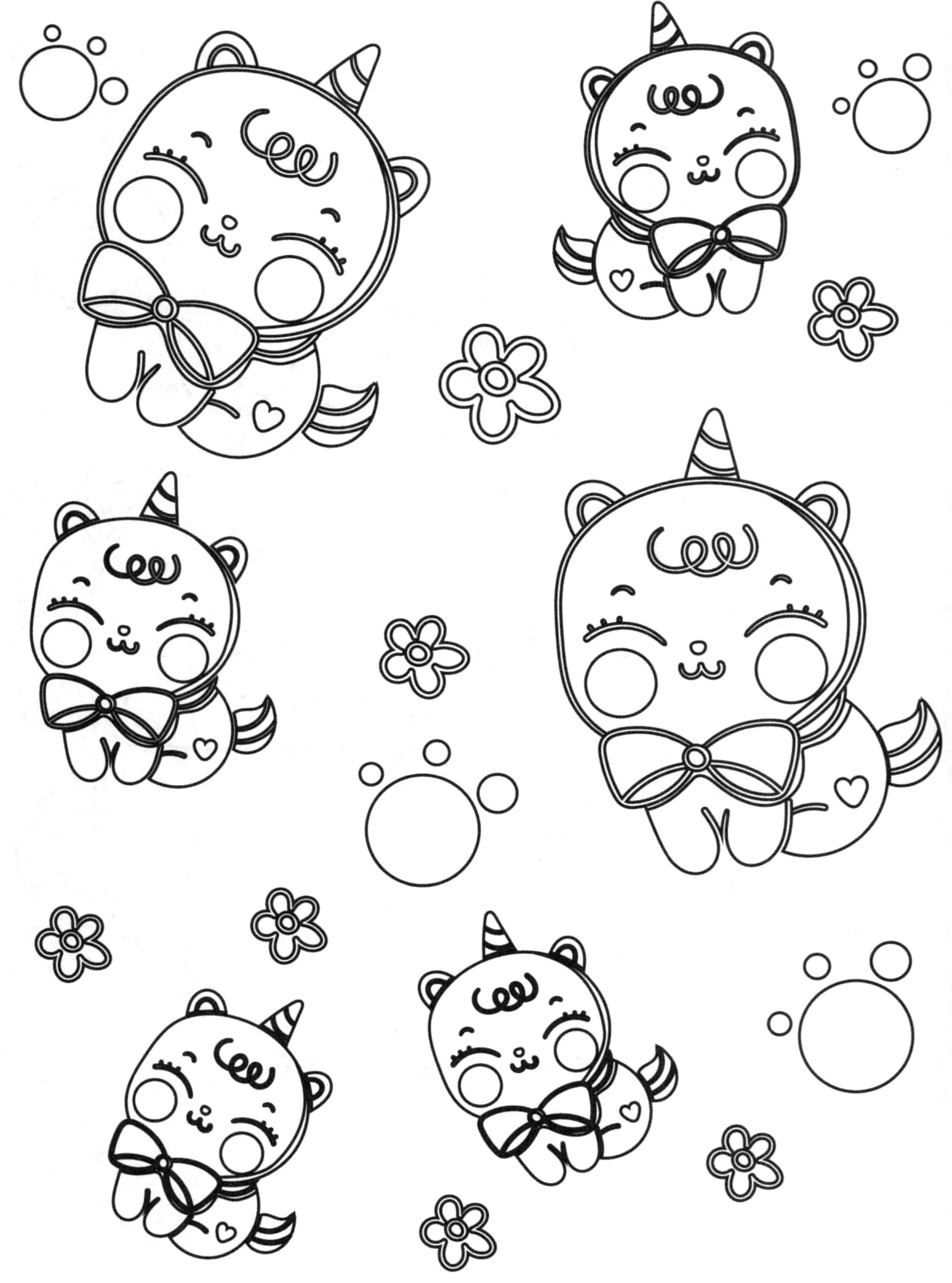

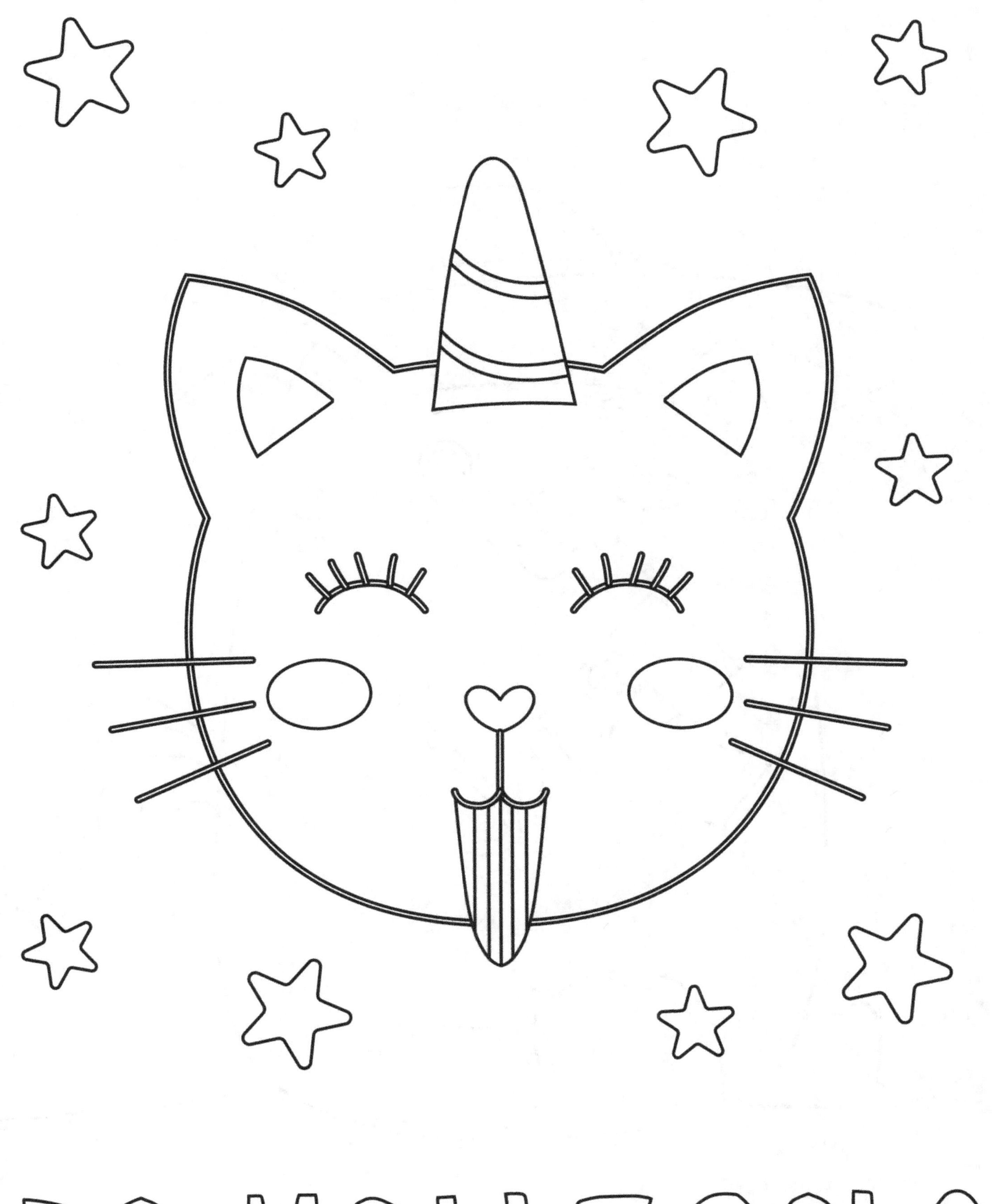

BE yourself

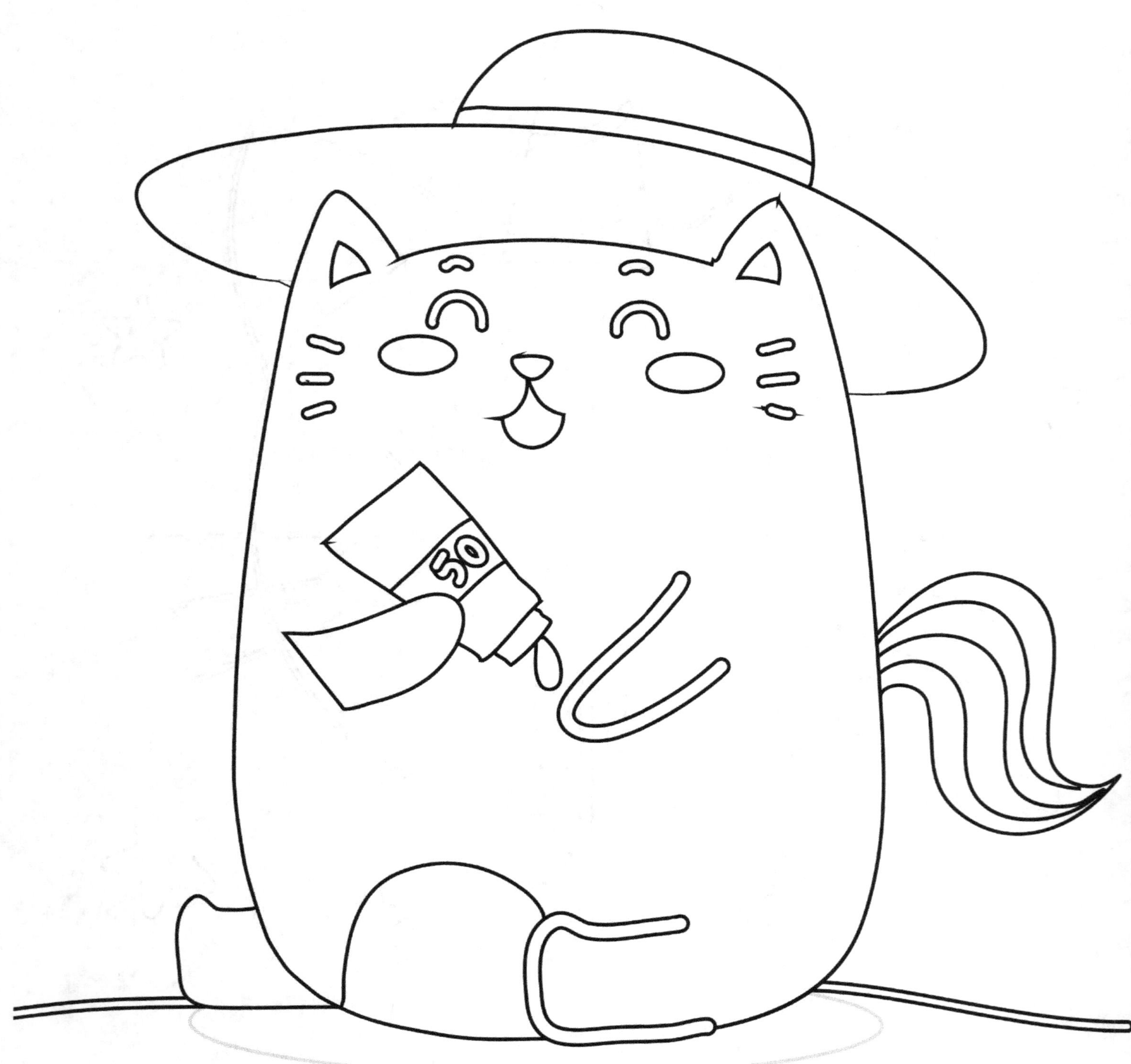
50

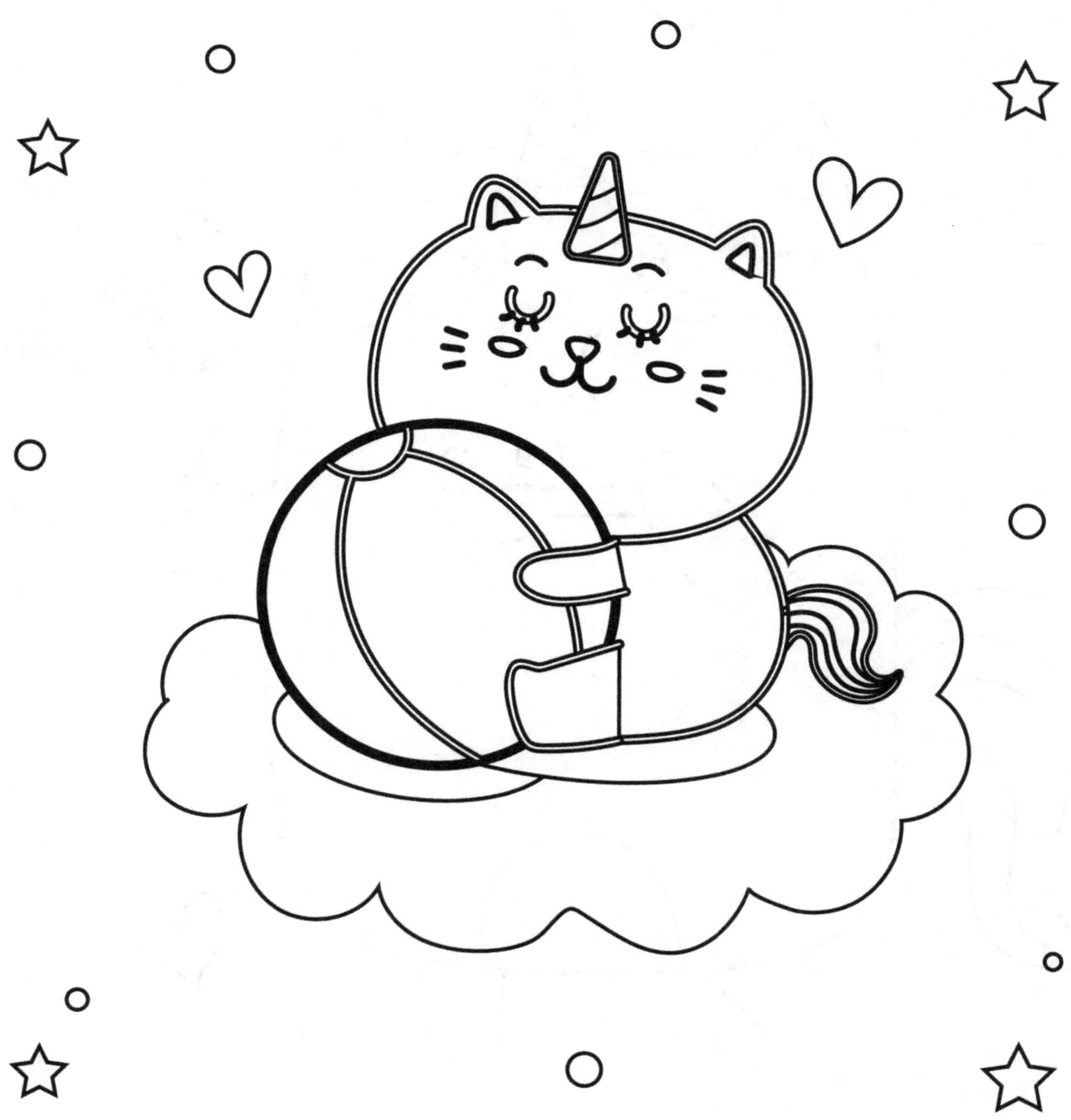

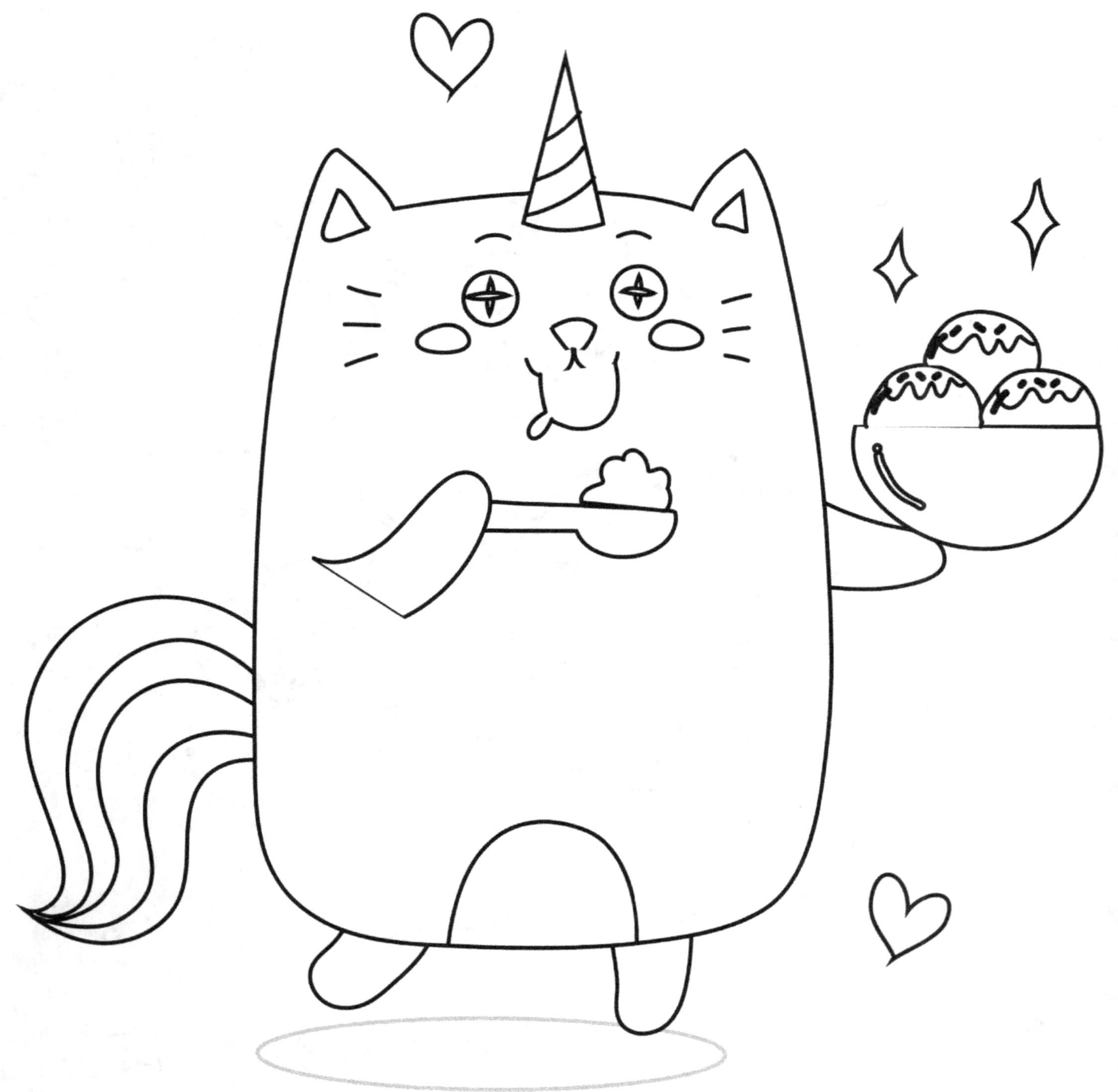

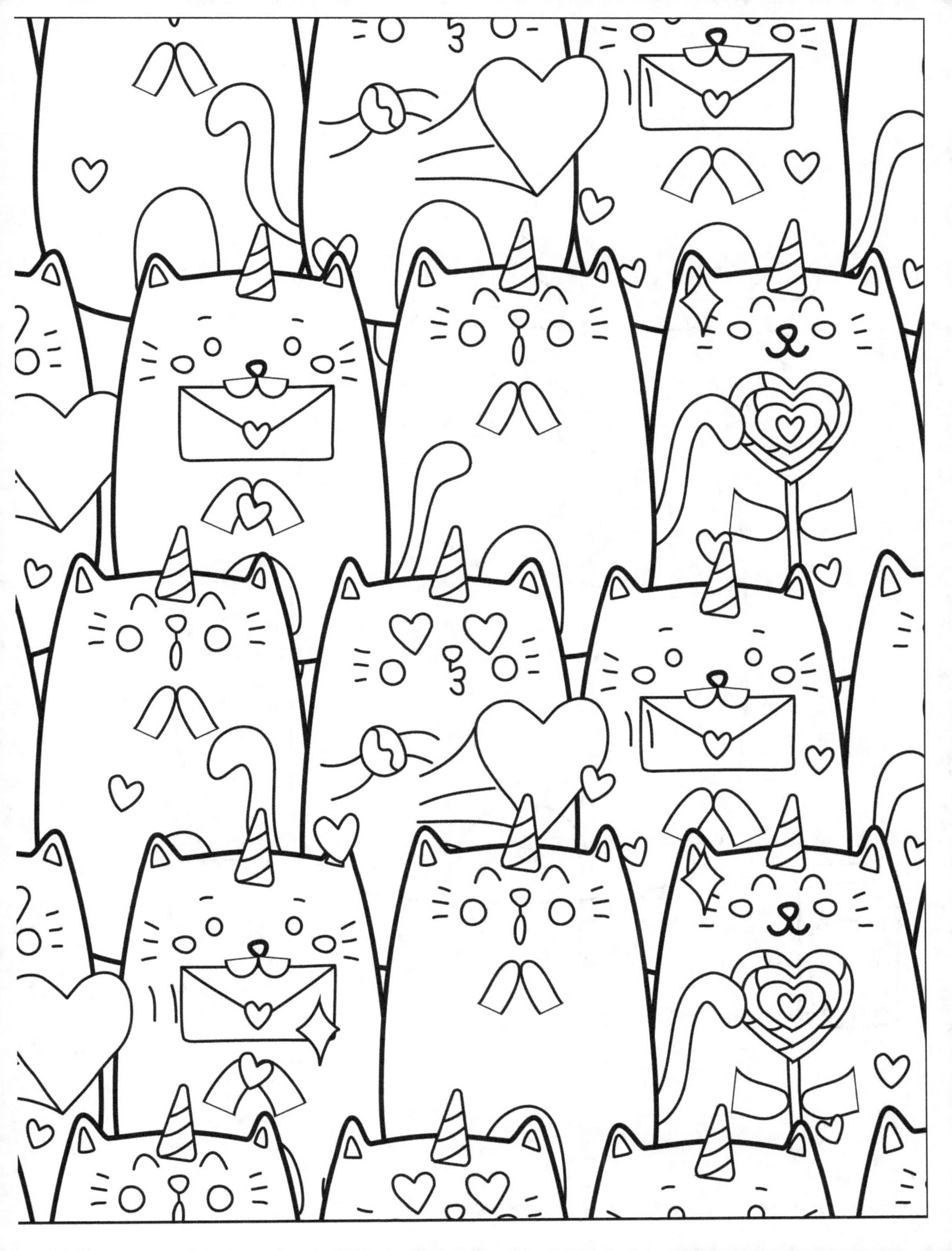

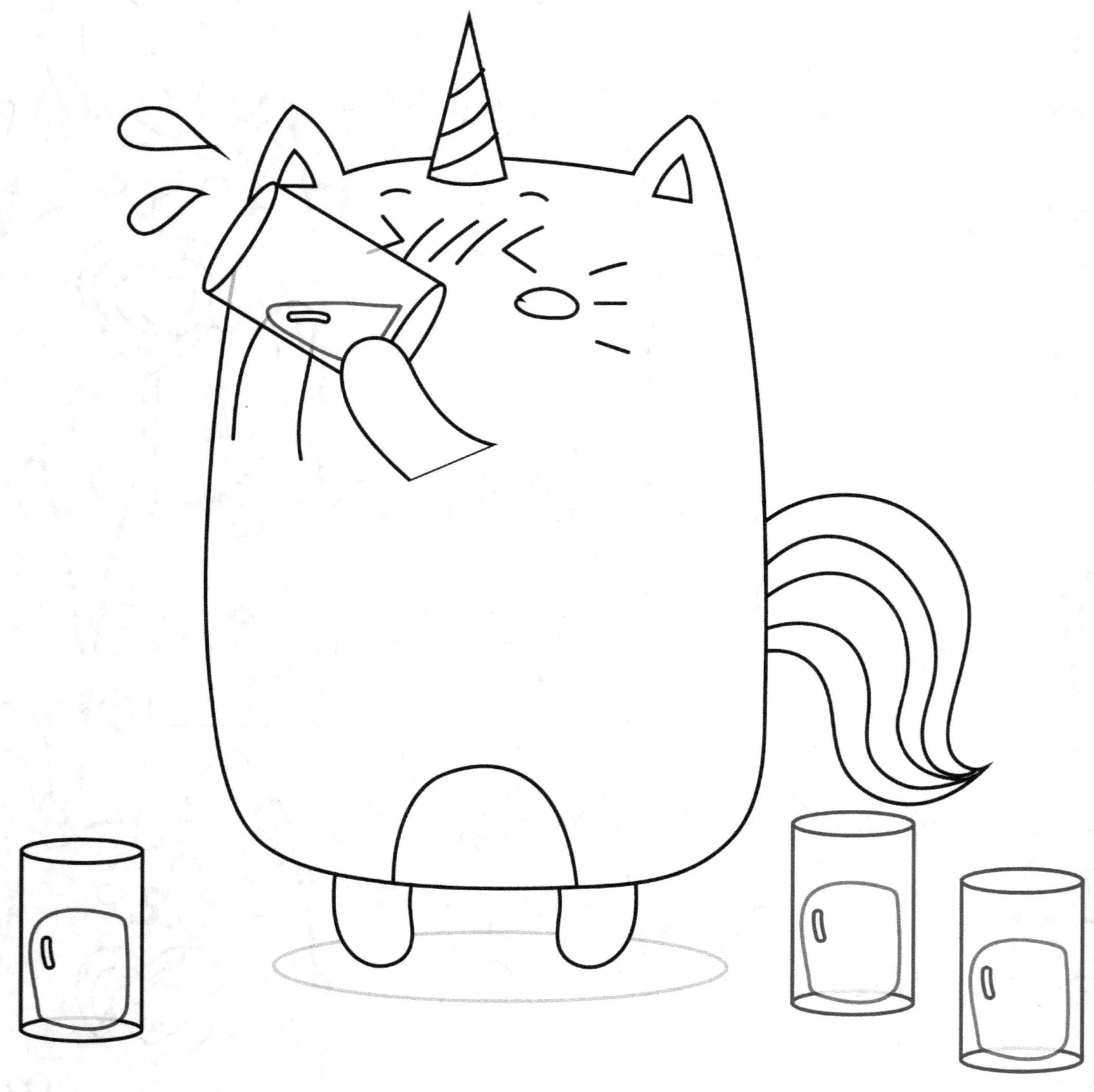

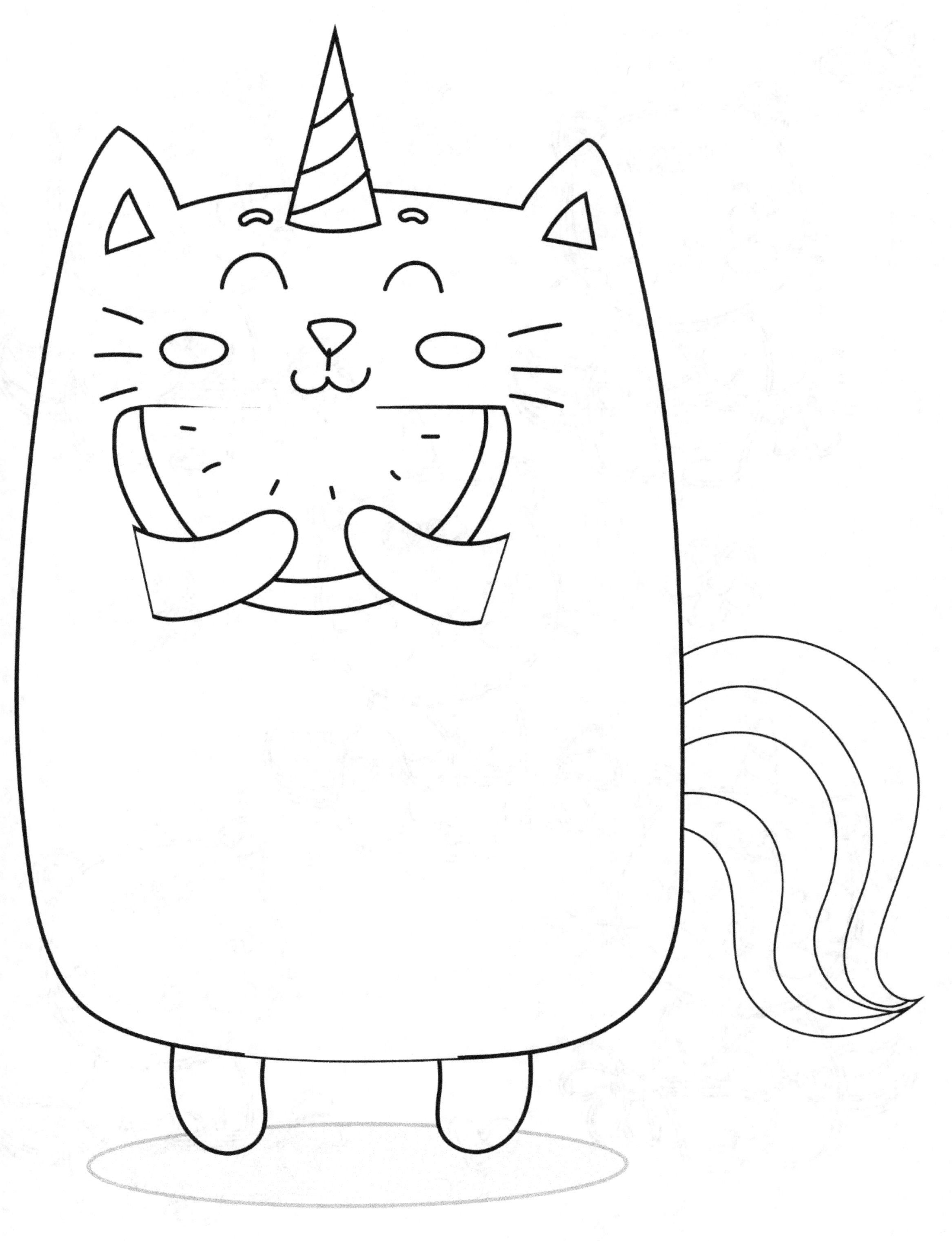

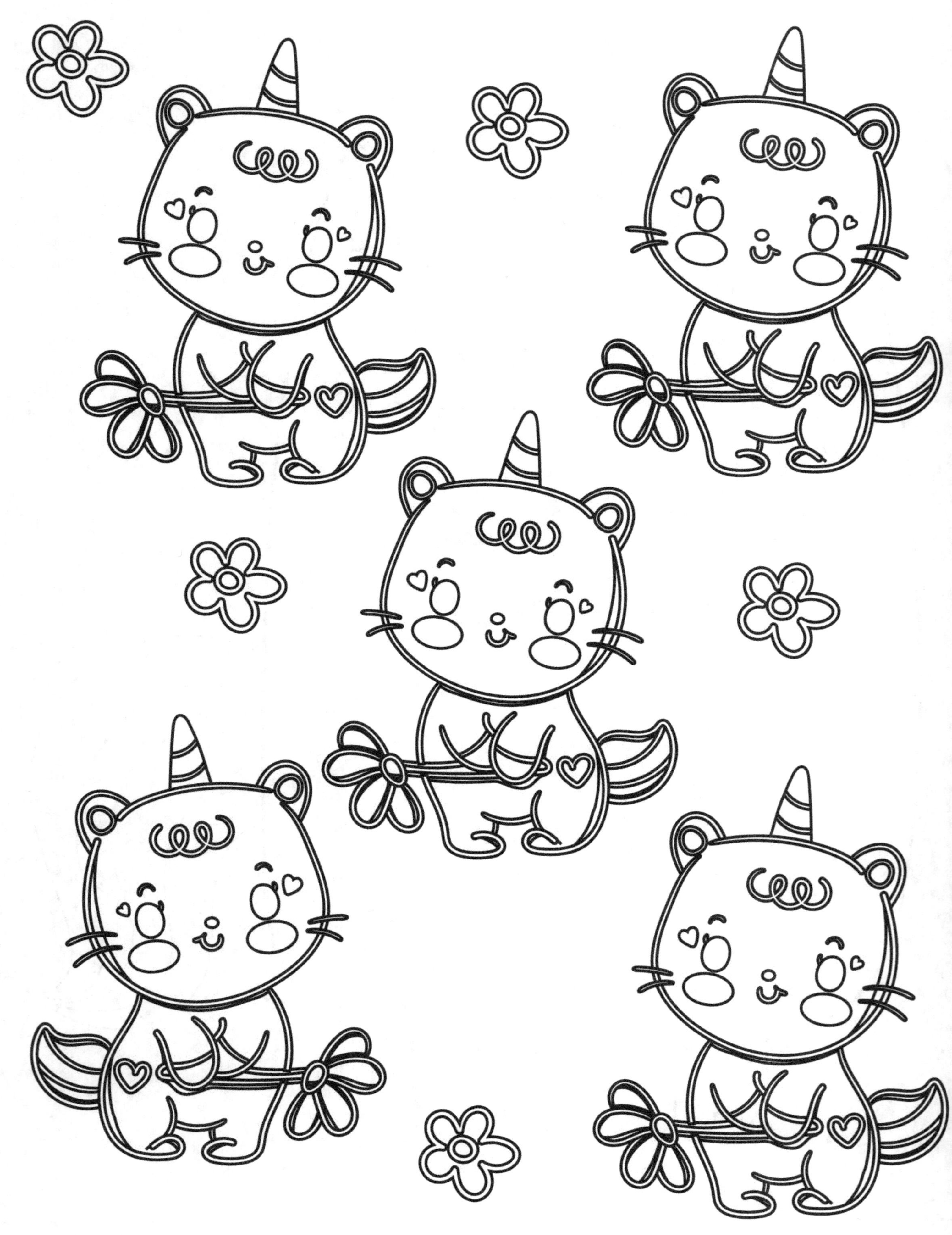

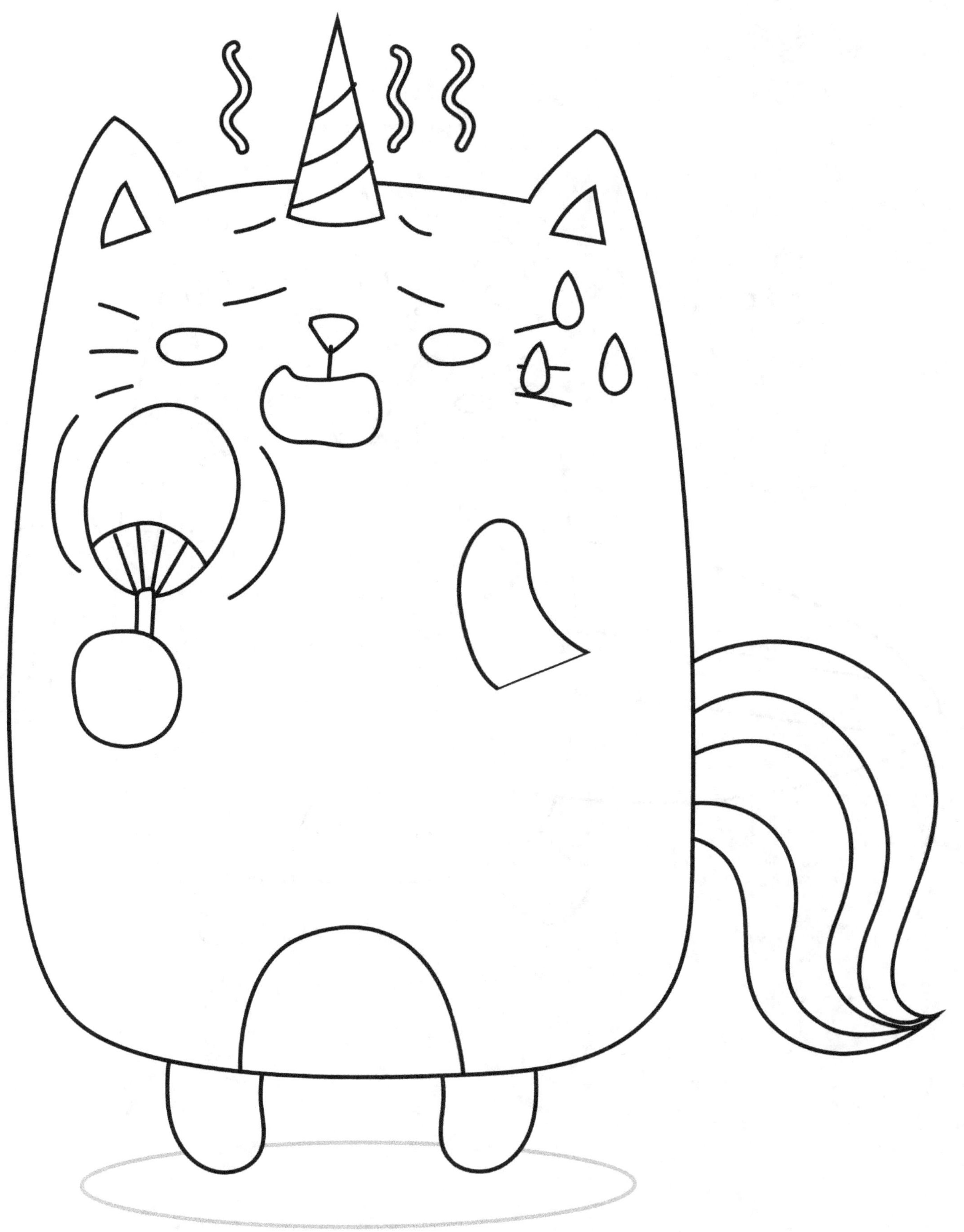

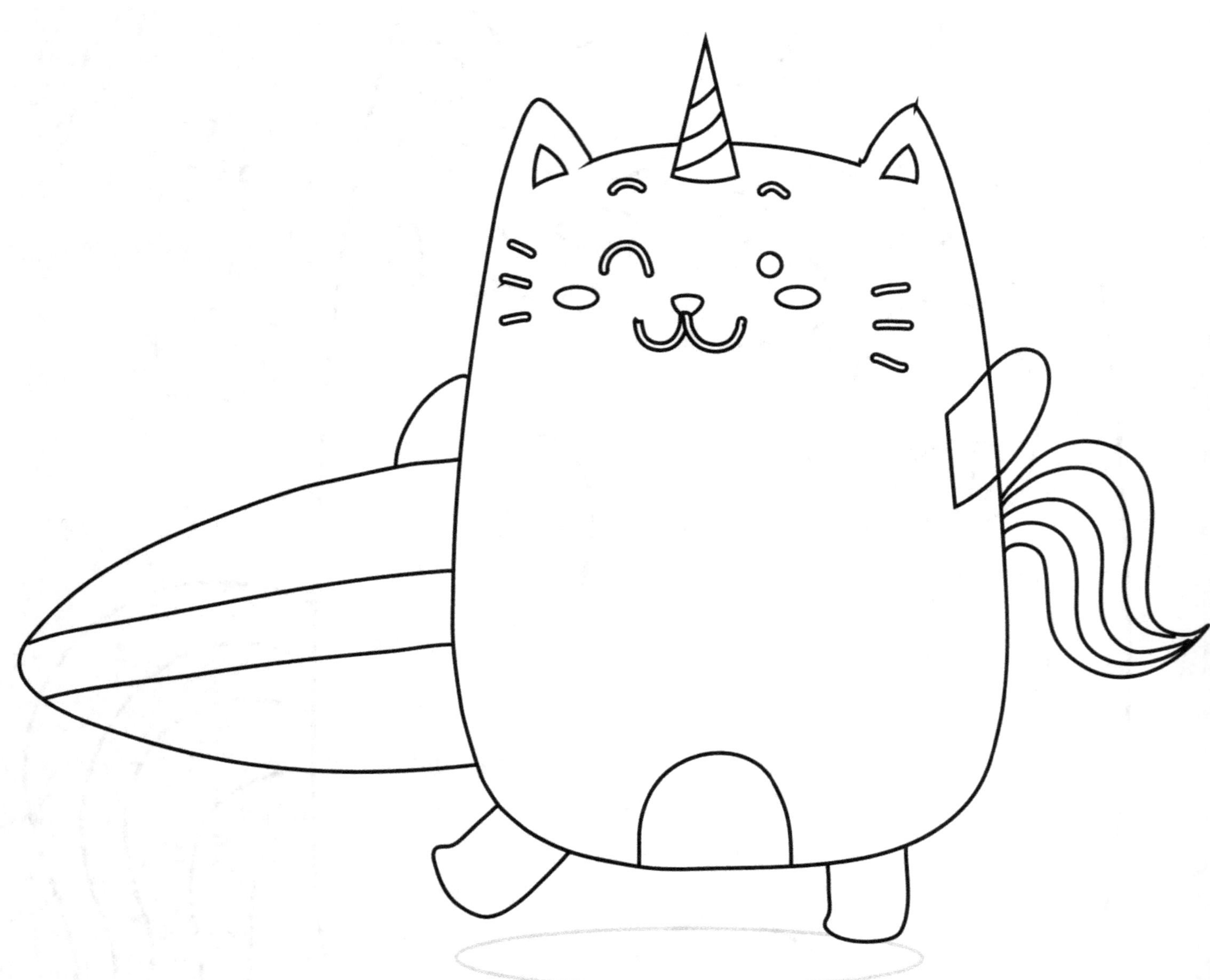

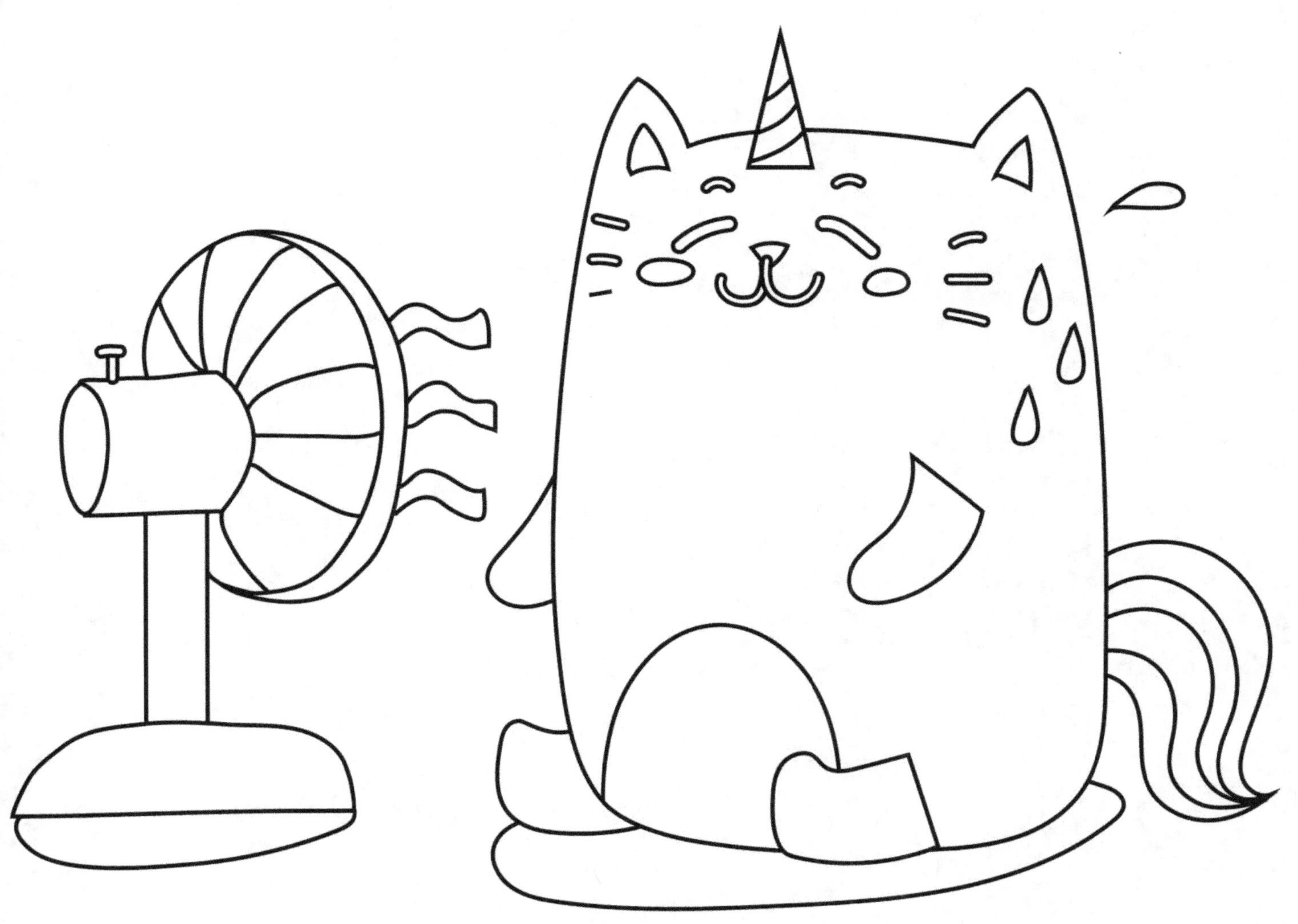

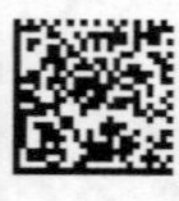